Original title:
Poetry in the Ponderosa

Copyright © 2025 Creative Arts Management OÜ
All rights reserved.

Author: Amelia Montgomery
ISBN HARDBACK: 978-1-80567-265-4
ISBN PAPERBACK: 978-1-80567-564-8

A Tapestry of Twisted Roots

In the forest where squirrels do roam,
A raccoon stole our pizza, oh where's the dome?
Trees twist and shout with a giggling glee,
While owls hoot, "Is that pizza just for me?"

Below the branches, a secret dance,
The mushrooms wear hats, they've taken a stance.
The winds whisper jokes that tickle the leaves,
While chipmunks debate what each other believes.

Poetic Breath of the Wilderness

In the heart where the wildflowers crack jokes,
The bees are the comedians, yes, they are folks!
With zany antics as they buzz all around,
Their poetry drips sweetly from flowers unbound.

A porcupine winks with a quill in his hand,
He claims he can juggle, but can't make a stand.
With every attempt, he gets stuck in the brush,
While the rabbits all chuckle and just watch the fuss.

Harmony in the High Branches

The crows barter gossip with flair in the sky,
As a skunk writes a symphony, oh my, oh my!
Each branch is a stage for the critters to play,
While the frogs hold the spotlight for an encore display.

With songs that are silly, they dance and they prance,
The fawns roll their eyes at the squirrels' wild chance.
As the wind carries laughter through leaves soft and bright,
The forest sings silly tunes all through the night.

Syllables in Secret Clearings

In whispers of shadows, the crickets all rhyme,
As the fireflies sparkle and dance in their prime.
The secrets of nature wrapped up in delight,
With punchlines that echo beneath silver light.

A fox pulls the pranks with a sneaky little grin,
While the owls roll their eyes, 'He's at it again!'
Every twig and each stone has a story to tell,
Of laughter and mischief, all woven so well.

The Untold Stories of Sylvan Shadows

In the woods where shadows dance,
Squirrels plot without a glance,
Chasing acorns, dodging trees,
Hiding secrets in the breeze.

The owls hoot with all their might,
Telling jokes that bring delight,
While pine cones chuckle, rolling free,
And teasing every passing bee.

Underneath the crescent moon,
Raccoons gather, one by one,
Sharing tales of daring feats,
And stealing crumbs from picnics, sweet.

The trees lean in, they want to know,
How many nuts can one squirrel throw?
While shadows giggle, full of glee,
In a forest party, wild and free.

The Verse of Verdant Vistas

In the fields where rabbits hop,
Squirrels dance and never stop.
The grass tickles all who dare,
While birds jest with a cheeky flair.

A deer sneezed, oh what a sight,
As it startled, took to flight.
The flowers giggle in the breeze,
And gossip with the bumblebees.

Mice wear hats, or so they say,
In the shade where they love to play.
Each tree whispers secrets bold,
Of silly tales from days of old.

Reflections in the Pondering Pines

A pine tree pondered what to wear,
Should it don a crown of hair?
The wind said, 'Oh, stick with green!'
'You're best when you're simply seen.'

Woodpeckers knock on tree trunks loud,
Announcing jokes to gather a crowd.
The sun giggles as it peeks,
At dancing shadows that tease and sneak.

A raccoon rolling down a hill,
Opted for silliness and thrill.
While owls wink with knowing eyes,
At all the antics in the skies.

Melodies in the Moonlit Grove

Under stars that twinkle bright,
Animals sing with pure delight.
A fox strummed on his tiny lute,
While a rabbit danced in a suit.

'Why chase the moon?' the badger said,
'When we can snack and laugh instead.'
Fireflies joined in with their light,
Creating chaos, oh what a night!

The moss took part, what a surprise,
Growing a beard of bright green ties.
As laughter echoed through the glade,
All of nature joyfully swayed.

Lines from the Leafy Voices

The leaves rustle with a chuckle,
As branches sway and do a shuffle.
The vines entwine in a playful spin,
While whispers tease about their kin.

A snail in shades, so very cool,
Declared, 'I'm the fastest of the fool!'
While ladybugs played tag on a stem,
As ants just sighed, 'We'll never win!'

In the thicket where shadows blend,
Critters argue over who's the friend.
And every twig has a tale to share,
With giggles echoing through the air.

The Language of Moss and Stone

Moss words whisper soft and low,
Stones chuckle at passersby,
A squirrel dances, wearing a bow,
While beetles gather for a pie.

The trees laugh, their branches wave,
A picnic of ants on a leaf,
The wind tries hard not to misbehave,
As grasshoppers share their brief grief.

Boulders nod with knowing grace,
The earth quakes with laughter's sound,
A ticklish breeze joins the race,
As nature's jokes spin round and round.

So listen close to the ground's jest,
Where moss and stone in glee conspire,
For even trees can blush and jest,
As life dances on, never tired.

Soliloquy in the Open Air

A breeze rolls in with a cheeky grin,
While daisies gossip nice and bright,
Clouds throw shade with a wink and spin,
As sunlight bursts in a playful fight.

A robin croons an off-key tune,
While birds trade puns in vibrant flight,
The sun dips low, a golden moon,
As squirrels debate what snack feels right.

Crickets chirp in fits of glee,
With fireflies making sparks that dance,
The world speaks in a breezy spree,
Encouraging all to take a chance.

In laughter wrapped, the world unfolds,
As wildflowers throw a garden party,
The air buzzes, and nature molds,
A comedy where all are hearty.

Nature's Canvas of Thought

Brushstrokes of leaves and skies so blue,
The artist here wears muddy shoes,
With splatters of laughter, a vibrant hue,
And bees buzzing tunes—a jolly muse.

Each flower's bloom, a punchline told,
A river giggles as it flows,
The mountains guard secrets of old,
While nature paints mischief as it goes.

A canvas of chaos, colors collide,
The owls wear glasses, reading at night,
While a cactus in boots goes for a ride,
In this gallery of quirky delight.

Here's nature's laughter in every frame,
A jester's wit in each leafy part,
The landscape grins, wild and untame,
Creating art with a fun-loving heart.

The Sigh of the Whispering Woods

In woods where giggles softly sigh,
Trees hold secrets in their rings,
Barking dogs join the witty high,
As owl's wisdom humorously clings.

The ferns stamp feet, a quiet dance,
While raccoons share a midnight snack,
Branches sway in a playful trance,
As shadows gather for a joke attack.

Under the moon's mischievous glow,
The whispers of leaves tickle the air,
A symphony of nature's show,
Where laughter lingers everywhere.

So listen close to the trees at play,
Embrace their zest in every fold,
For in their sighs, they gently say,
That life in the woods is pure gold.

Glistening Words in the Wilderness

In the woods where squirrels chat,
Words bounce like a playful cat.
Trees giggle with leafy delight,
As rhymes take flight in morning light.

A chipmunk dons a tiny tie,
Reciting stanzas with a sigh.
The brook joins in, a bubbly tune,
While birds chirp verses 'neath the moon.

Branches shake with laughter bright,
In this forest, all feels right.
Every rustle sings a line,
Nature's prance, oh how divine!

Acorns join the merry scene,
Dancing on the grass so green.
In this haven, joy unfurled,
A silly symphony, life twirled.

Soliloquy of Shadows

Shadows waltz upon the glade,
Echoes of laughter, never afraid.
A wise old owl hoots rhymes at night,
While crickets chirp with all their might.

Mice in hats, a fine soirée,
In the moonlight, they prance and play.
Each whisper from the forest floor,
Unfolds a comedy to explore.

Beneath the stars, a play takes place,
With shadows miming every grace.
The laughter folds like silken sheets,
As the world turns with heart-skipping beats.

At dawn, the sun begins to bloom,
Awakening the merry room.
Nature's actors take their bow,
In this whispered show – oh wow!

Epiphany Among the Evergreens

In the pines, a thought took flight,
Dancing like a feathered kite.
Needles tickle, thoughts abound,
As wisdom waits without a sound.

The squirrels plan their big retreat,
While poets jot down gentle tweets.
An antlered friend joins with a grin,
Saying, "Let's rhyme, it's where we begin!"

Amidst the trunks, a giggle swells,
Stories swirling like old spells.
Every twist of bark and leaf,
Brings hilarity and belief.

With laughter echoing through the trees,
Each moment sways like the breeze.
In evergreens, our tales ignite,
Bright endings that just feel so right.

The Listeners Beneath the Canopy

Beneath the leaves, they gather round,
Antlers bobbing, all abound.
The wisdom of the forest speaks,
In giggles, chuckles, mellow peaks.

Bunnies tap dance to the beat,
While crickets play their crowd-pleasing feat.
Each laughing breeze a soft embrace,
In this hidden, joyous place.

The sun dips low, a glowing grin,
As shadows join the merry din.
Every whisper in the air,
Holds secrets that we all can share.

So if you wander, take a seat,
Join the friends where laughter's sweet.
The canopy, our theater grand,
Where joy and humor go hand in hand.

Ballads Born from Bark

In the forest, trees might sing,
A squirrel's dance, a silly fling.
Their shadows twist, their branches sway,
Nature's comedy on display.

With every knot, a tale unspooled,
Of acorns lost and squirrels fooled.
The roots hold secrets, giggles contained,
While leaves are rattling, uncontained.

Oh, bark is thick but humor's rich,
A woodpecker's tap, a clever hitch.
The wind whispers jokes, just listen near,
While pinecones chuckle, never fear.

At dusk, the critters tell their jest,
The forest floor, a humor fest.
With every rustle, laughter blooms,
In leafy halls and shady rooms.

Stanzas in the Sutures of Nature

There's a cactus that wears a goofy hat,
A tortoise tripping over a mat.
Bees doing ballet, quite the sight,
While owls play cards, well into night.

The rivers chuckle as they flow,
While fish strut by, putting on a show.
Each ripple holds a punchline clear,
The frogs croak laughter for all to hear.

Branches swing, a monkey's grin,
Nature's stand-up, let the fun begin!
The stars above join in the spree,
While crickets sing in perfect glee.

Among the bushes, riddles bloom,
A hedgehog spins tales, dispelling gloom.
With each rustle, giggles arise,
Nature's humor wears a disguise.

The Musings That Fluttered

A butterfly flutters, in silly loops,
Chasing its tail amongst clucking croups.
The daisies giggle, bowing with grace,
While the daisies poke fun at a snail's pace.

The sparrows gossip, chirp a rhyme,
Over a worm, what a great time!
With every flap, a snicker shared,
Birds weave stories, none of them bared.

The wind plays pranks, tickles the trees,
A raccoon wears a mask, oh, what a tease!
Nature's jesters, every nook,
Promising giggles on every hook.

Amidst the flowers, chuckles blend,
While nature dances, always a friend.
With petals bright and hearts aglow,
Humor in bloom, a constant flow.

Oaths of the Old Growth

The wise old oaks, standing tall,
Sworn to laughter, never to fall.
Their stories twist, they poke and prod,
As squirrels debate, 'Who's the real god?'

Worn by time, their bark may crack,
But humor's shield keeps them on track.
A woodpecker's peck sends everyone reeling,
Nature's punchline, oh, what a feeling!

With acorns rolling, a visual jest,
The stumps laugh loud, 'We are the best!'
As branches wave in playful fray,
The forest giggles through every day.

In twilight's glow, shadows take shape,
With vines that twist like a comic cape.
Oaths in the woods, treasured and bright,
Nature's amusement, our pure delight.

Whims of the Whispering Wind

A squirrel's chitter rings so clear,
It shouts to neighbors, 'Come over here!'
With acorns bounced, they start to dance,
A jolly flash in nature's trance.

The breeze brings giggles through the trees,
As leaves perform their silly pleas.
A gentle push, then down they spiral,
In a leafy shindig, all in trial.

A rabbit joins, a hop so spry,
While butterflies just flit on by.
What a show, this woodland spree,
With whispers of joy, wild and free!

When dusk arrives, they'll take a break,
And gather 'round to share a cake.
With candlelight from lightning bugs,
They laugh and munch on sweet nut hugs.

Ethereal Echoes of Earth

In the meadow, a cow sings low,
Moo-ing rhythms that steal the show.
Grasshoppers join with their chirpy sound,
An enchanting band in blue skies found.

A goat thinks he's a rock star bright,
Climbing high to reach new heights.
But tumbles down, a comedic spree,
He gets up laughing, 'Look at me!'

The flowers giggle in hues so bold,
Sharing secrets they've never told.
Their petals dance, a silly ballet,
Tickled by breezes that sway and play.

As the sun sets, the jokes draw near,
With every chuckle, the stars appear.
Night blankets the whimsy we spun,
Whispers of mirth, day is done.

Folded Wishes Beneath the Branches

Beneath the boughs, a secret pact,
Where dreams and naps are smoothly stacked.
A cat naps on a book of lore,
While squirrels argue over nuts galore.

Twinkling lights in firefly formations,
Paint the dark with shining creations.
They giggle as they zip and zap,
In this world, a cozy lap.

The wise old owl serves jokes in night,
With punchlines that bring pure delight.
His hoots ring out a merry sound,
And laughter resonates all around.

When morning breaks, the fun returns,
With sunny rays, the mischief burns.
Each wish folded, from heart to tree,
In breezy whispers, we all are free.

Poetic Pathways Through the Pines

On winding trails, the pine trees chuckle,
As critters bustle with a sudden shuffle.
A chubby hedgehog rolls down a hill,
And the giggles echo, rat-a-tat thrill!

Raccoons in masks hold a late-night fiesta,
Stealing snacks like sneaky siesta.
With moonlit games and giggly pranks,
The woodland friends form joyful ranks.

A racquet of leaves, a skipping beat,
Underfoot where pinecones greet.
Laughter rings in the cool pine air,
With every step, jokes to share.

As twilight falls, they gather 'round,
For stories of silliness renowned.
With warmth and cheer, they all align,
On paths of fun, along the pine.

Chronicles of the Pine Cone

A pine cone rolled right down the hill,
It crashed into a squirrel's meal.
The squirrel looked up, eyes round and wide,
"Was that my snack?" it squeaked with pride.

The cone just laughed, bounced back with glee,
"Not today, friend. I'm wild and free!"
But tripped on roots, went spinning fast,
And landed right where the flowers last.

The flowers giggled under the sun,
"Oh look! A cone! Let's have some fun!"
They danced and swayed in the breeze so bright,
As the cone joined in, what a funny sight!

Now pine cones know, it's best not to roam,
Lest they find a wildflower making a home!
With laughter and sunshine, they all agree,
Nature's a circus, just wait and see!

Echoing Footfalls of Time

Footfalls echo on a forest path,
A raccoon's snicker, a sly little laugh.
He tiptoes around with a hat too big,
Claiming he's off to a dance or a gig.

A deer nearby, with curious ears,
Said, "Watch your step, avoid the sneers!"
But the raccoon just spun like a funky star,
"I'm now the prince of the pinecone bazaar!"

The trees swayed with a chuckling sound,
At the antics of critters dancing round.
The shadows laughed as the sun grew dim,
In this grand old forest, none could be grim.

Then came a bear, with two left feet,
He tripped on a root, a clumsy defeat.
Yet the echoing laughter would never fade,
In the heart of the woods, memories are made!

Reverie in the Shaded Glade

In the glade where shadows play,
A rabbit wobbled, hip-hip-hooray!
He missed his mark, a big ol' hop,
And landed plop in a puddle—kerplop!

The frogs croaked tales of great delight,
As the rabbit splashed, what a silly sight!
"You should stick to tunnels, friend dear,
Leave jumping to us, it's crystal clear!"

With a shake and shiver, the rabbit jumped out,
Covered in mud, he laughed and pouted.
The sunlight glittered, laughter was free,
In the glade of giggles, all hearties agree!

So next time you visit this shady nook,
Watch the rabbits before you look!
For fun finds a way to sparkle and shine,
In the heart of the fun, where tall willow twines.

The Artistry of the Wildflowers

Wildflowers twirled in a color parade,
Each shade a giggle, each petal displayed.
The daisies debated whose scent was the best,
While poppies snoozed, enjoying their rest.

A dandelion sent wishes afloat,
But a passing bee thought it was a joke.
"Are you putting me to work?" it exclaimed,
"I was just here for the nectar, not fame!"

Then came the sun with a chuckle so bright,
"Don't grumble, dear bee, you'll take flight tonight!"
With a buzz of delight, they all shared their roles,
Each bloom and bee filled with laughter in souls.

So if you wander through fields full of cheer,
Remember the blooms hold laughter quite dear.
They know the secrets of joy and play,
In petals and pollen, the wildflowers sway!

Reflections on the Edge of Dawn

In the early light, I trip on dew,
My coffee's cold, but my heart feels new.
A squirrel mocks, with acorn in hand,
While I search for sleep, in this waking land.

My worries float like leaves in a stream,
Too busy now to chase that old dream.
The robins gossip, the sun starts to chuckle,
As I dodge a bee – oh, what a struggle!

The shadows stretch, they play hide and seek,
A worm tells tales of the day that's bleak.
But laughter rings in the morning's embrace,
Nature's jesters all keep up the pace.

With each little giggle, I'm caught in the swirl,
Dancing with dandelions, giving life a twirl.
In this morning calm, fun knows no bounds,
Life's silly surprises are all around.

Musings Under Starlit Veils

Beneath the vastness, my thoughts take flight,
Counting critters that dance in the night.
A raccoon winks, with a sly little grin,
While I wonder if life's just a game to win.

The owls hoot secrets, the frogs sing a tune,
As I ponder if the moon can play a cartoon.
Mice gather close, sharing snacks for the night,
In this cosmic laughter, everything feels right.

Giggles escape, like fireflies in flight,
I'm lost in their rhythm, oh what a sight!
Against the backdrop where dreams like to play,
Even the stars join in on this fray.

Culture appears in the clatter and chime,
As night means mischief, no reason, no rhyme.
Under celestial glow, I burst into glee,
Who knew that the universe loved company?

Shadows That Speak

In the twilight dance, shadows boast tales,
Of mischief and giggles that never grow stale.
A tree leans close, swaps stories of yore,
While the creek laughs softly, telling more.

Mice plan a heist on some crumbs long lost,
They scurry along, oh, what a cost!
And in the dark, I hear whispers and cheer,
As shadows unfold all the joys hidden near.

The lonesome lamp flickers, bees pluck at fate,
While I juggle my snacks and contemplate.
Points to ponder in the cool evening air,
Where laughter's the currency, beyond compare.

In every corner, there's mischief and jest,
Nature's critics never seem to rest.
I'll join the parade, where shadows collide,
With my own little quips, I shall not hide.

Nature's Silent Resonance

Among the tall trunks, nature's heartbeat sings,
Echoes of laughter, oh the joy it brings.
A chipmunk performs, its antics absurd,
While I scribble nonsense, not one word heard.

In the rustle of leaves, there's a chuckle or two,
As the branches sway with a comedic view.
The grass tickles toes and brings out a snort,
In this raucous realm, we don't need a court.

Under soft breezes, the petals confide,
Sharing whispered jokes, on a soft-watered ride.
A worm wears a crown, how regal, I'd say,
If only we all could laugh this way.

From the tiniest bug to the grandest of trees,
All gather around, partaking in ease.
Nature's confessions bring giggles untamed,
In this silent symphony, we're all entertained.

Secret Histories in the Leaf Litter

Amidst the crunch, a tale unfolds,
Squirrels gossip, their secrets told.
A dance of ants in a conga line,
Nature's humor, oh so divine.

A toad in shades, looking quite chic,
Winks at the sun, playfully sleek.
Mud puddles laugh, splashing with glee,
As worms tell jokes beneath the tree.

A leaf falls, with a crinkled grin,
Whispers of mischief, ready to spin.
They say the roots have their own league,
With meetings held near the old twig.

So listen close, when you stroll by,
For nature's lore is not a lie.
In every crackle, the jesters play,
Leaf litter tales, hip-hip-hooray!

Illuminated Lines of Life

Sunlight spills on the grassy stage,
Where rabbits read from a dusty page.
With comical rhymes that twist and twine,
The wind rolls laughter, oh so fine.

A butterfly slips, almost a fall,
While bees in bowties buzz one and all.
They argue sweets in a comical fight,
With punchlines that tickle, what a delight!

The trees lean in, their branches a stir,
Hearing the tale of each jolly blur.
With giggles exchanged among the vine,
Life's quirks expressed, so very divine.

So take a seat 'neath the twinkling leaves,
As nature spins tales, one never leaves.
Each illuminated line brings a grin,
In this wild world where fun's a win!

Nature's Quill Among the Quaking Aspens

An aspen quakes, laughing with glee,
As wind tells stories, wild and free.
A squirrel types with a tiny paw,
On bark that's blushing, oh what a flaw!

"Once I saw a pine in a dance,"
The moose chuckles, giving a glance.
With twirls and spins, oh what a sight,
Nature's ballet, a true delight!

Frogs croak rhythm, a quirky tune,
While shadows waltz beneath the moon.
Nature's quill pens each silly tale,
As the crickets sing their nightly scale.

So stroll through woods of whimsy and cheer,
Where laughter echoes for all to hear.
In every rustle, a giggle's spun,
With each quaking aspen, the fun's never done!

The Ballad of Burgeoning Boughs

The boughs stretch wide, dreaming of heights,
While squirrels host parties in breezy nights.
With acorns in hand, they raise a cheer,
To tales of mischief that all can hear.

Chirps and tweets fill the air with fun,
As blue jays squawk, outshining the sun.
The branches sway to a jig so spry,
While roots below let out a sigh.

Leaves flutter down, like confetti so bright,
Creating laughter in soft morning light.
A badger in bowler, tiptoes about,
In search of the punchline, there is no doubt.

With every gust, the stories unfold,
Of wise old trees and their antics bold.
The ballad plays under the vast, blue sky,
A charming concert where quirks abide!

Treasury of Timbered Thoughts

In a grove where the trees all sneeze,
A squirrel shimmies with such ease.
He gathers acorns, makes a fuss,
While pine cones tumble with a rush.

Each branch holds secrets, tales of yore,
A woodpecker knocks, asking for more.
Yet when the wind starts to play,
The trees just laugh and sway away.

With roots that tickle and branches that dance,
Every critter here takes a chance.
They swap tall tales from limb to root,
While rhymes bloom bright like morning fruit.

So join the fun, there's much to glean,
In this quirky forest scene.
For in every rustle, chirp, and chime,
Lies a treasure trove of silly rhyme.

The Poetry of the Perpetual Pine

Oh evergreen, with needles so bright,
You sway and dance day and night.
With each passing breeze, you elegantly twirl,
Causing chaos in every squirrel.

Your bark is rough, your jokes are sly,
You whisper secrets as birds fly by.
Under your shade, even shadows play,
Creating a scene that's wild and gay.

When it rains, you wear a moody hat,
Complaining softly, while sparrows chat.
Yet come the sun, you prance and preen,
What a comical sight, a leafy queen!

So in this wood, let laughter reign,
With your tales of suns and drops of rain.
From every branch, a chuckle to share,
In this laughter-filled atmosphere.

Lark's Lament in the Leafy Shade

A lark sits perched, a bit bemused,
In the leafy green, feeling a little confused.
He opens his beak, but what comes out?
A giggle, a snort, then a hearty shout!

With worms as friends, and bugs for laughs,
He starts to recite his silly drafts.
In every turn and flutter, he finds
A way to tickle the tree's own minds.

The breeze weighs in, it can't help but jeer,
As the leaves giggle softly, lending an ear.
The forest joins in the daily jest,
Finding humor in their leafy nest.

So here's to the lark, who won't let gloom,
Disturb the joy that fills the room.
With every chirp, the world gets bright,
In the playful shade, everything feels right.

Dreamscapes Under the Ancient Boughs

Beneath the boughs, where shadows play,
A dreamer lounges at the end of day.
With wild ideas and thoughts so grand,
He drifts away to a far-off land.

Where squirrels can dance like ballerinas,
And frogs wear crowns made of hyacinth.
The trees, they clap with gnarled old hands,
As laughter echoes across the lands.

Each branch a bridge to whimsical things,
A turtle recites while the woodpecker sings.
The whole forest joins in a jig,
That tickles the toes of the sleeping pig.

So come take a seat on the mossy floor,
Where dreams and giggles just never bore.
In this realm where the funny blooms,
Life feels sweeter amidst the tunes.

Verses at Sunset's Edge

A raccoon wore a hat quite fine,
He danced and pranced, a sight divine.
The sun dipped low, the sky ablaze,
The critters joined in sunset rays.

A squirrel stole a peanut prize,
Then tripped and fell with silly cries.
The laughter rang through trees so tall,
As shadows played their twilight sprawl.

A bird hummed tunes of pure delight,
While fireflies flickered, oh what a sight!
With giggles echoing through the glade,
They formed a dance that never stayed.

So gather round this comical show,
Where nature's mishaps shine and glow.
At sunset's edge, where joy prevails,
We'll spin our tales on gentle trails.

The Language of Trees

The trees gossip in rustling leaves,
"Told you so!" the old oak heaves.
Birch trees tremble with mischievous glee,
Spinning tales under roots, quite free.

Pine trees chuckle when gusts come by,
"Is that the wind or your breath?" they sigh.
The maples giggle, their branches sway,
As squirrels bounce in a nut-filled fray.

A willow whispers to the creek,
"Oak is grumpy, just too antique!"
So different yet all share a laugh,
In nature's book, a single graph.

So listen close to leafy jest,
Where pines poke fun and spruces jest.
In this woodland of whimsy, mischief roams,
Crafting stories that feel like home.

Starlit Sylvan Serenades

Under the stars, a raccoon's tunes,
He strums his banjo, shaking the dunes.
Owls hoot in rhythm, frogs keep the beat,
While crickets chirp in a soft, sweet heat.

A fox in a bow tie joins the affair,
Dancing in circles, without a care.
The moon beams down, a spotlight true,
On this wild show, a midnight view.

A bear plays maracas, shaking with pride,
While badgers play cards, hoping to hide.
"Who's got the ace?" they whisper with glee,
As constellations wink from each tree.

So gather 'round, and take a seat,
The forest is lively, a wondrous treat.
In starlit nights, when laughter's grand,
Join in the fun, hand in hand!

Echoes of the Pine Forest

In the pine forest, echoes call,
Sounds of giggles bounce off the wall.
A deer in a tutu prances bright,
Trying to twirl in the fading light.

"Catch me if you can!" a raccoon shouts,
As pinecones rain, the woodland routs.
The wind whispers secrets, oh so sly,
While saplings snicker as they wave goodbye.

A bear and a badger go toe to toe,
In a dance-off with moves that glow.
The crowd of critters gathers around,
Cheering and howling as laughter abound.

So wander deep, embrace the mirth,
In this pine forest full of worth.
Where echoes linger, joy cascades,
And every step has memories made.

Songbird Serenades in the Tree Tops

A bird with a hat sings loud and clear,
His pitch is a banquet, we all draw near.
With twirls and with flips, he prances with glee,
Each note is a laugh, come join for some tea.

Squirrels join in with their own little tune,
Doing the cha-cha beneath the bright moon.
The owl rolls his eyes, not into this game,
But secretly wishes he too could be famed.

The breeze brings confetti, leaves dancing about,
The song of the tree tops, oh what a shout!
Each critter a star, it's a marvelous sight,
As evening unfolds, we dance into night.

With laughter and chirps, the air fills with cheer,
As everyone's welcome—come gather right here!
In the orchestra's chaos, we find blissful fun,
Who knew nature's concert could be this well done?

The Breath of Ancient Roots

Roots tangled and twisted, like stories well told,
Whispering secrets of times far and old.
The trees throw a party, inviting the ants,
For beetles in tuxes are doing their dances.

Mice in a corner, with cheese and a grin,
Play cards with the fox, a daring sly win.
Each root has a tale, filled with jest and cheer,
You'd laugh if you heard, but the branches just leer.

The crickets all chirp, with their drill sergeant flair,
A lineup of nonsense fills up the cool air.
The owls, wise and stern, grumble "Keep it down!"
But giggles keep rising, they can't wear a frown.

So next time you're walking near trees hushed and stout,
Just listen for laughter, they're having a bout.
With roots deeply planted, the fun will not cease,
Join in on the mirth; let your worries release.

Whispers of Pine and Ink

Pine trees are poets, their needles like quills,
Scribbling in silence, they capture their thrills.
With every soft whisper, a rhyme takes its flight,
In the shadows of pines, ideas ignite.

A squirrel fetches acorns, his props in the show,
He juggles and tumbles, putting on quite a flow.
The crooked old cedar just chuckles away,
Leaving ink blobs of laughter for all to convey.

With sap like a fountain, the verses do pour,
Each squirrel instinctively steps out for an encore.
The laughs grow like branches, oh what a delight,
For nature's own scribes now dance in the light.

So next time you wander 'neath pines standing tall,
Just listen for giggles; you'll hear through it all.
The whispers of muses, their quills in a spin,
Creating a world where the fun will begin.

Songs Beneath the Conifers

Beneath the tall conifers, the critters conspire,
They gather in circles, with jest they conspire.
A raccoon in shades spins a tale of the night,
While chipmunks take bets on who'll win in this fight.

The porcupine laughs, "You have no such chance!
You're all just line dancers who can't even prance!"
The weasel, with wit sharper than his quills,
Tells them that laughter is what truly thrills.

With acorns as maracas, the song starts to swell,
Each voice, a sweet melody, ringing like a bell.
A chorus erupts as the pine needles sway,
The forest bustles with joy, come join the ballet!

So if you should wander where the conifers grow,
Join in on the fun, let the good times flow.
With comedy woven in nature's embrace,
The songs will keep echoing, time cannot erase.

Lament in the Land of Tall Shadows

A squirrel stole my sandwich today,
He laughed as he scampered away.
I shouted, 'Hey, that's not fair!'
But he just twitched his fluffy hair.

The crows cawed loud, a raucous sound,
As they peered at me from branches around.
I offered them crumbs, a peace sign,
But they squawked, 'Why waste your good time?'

The owls winked from their lofty spy,
While I stood below and wondered why.
Nature's a jester, in breezy disguise,
With all of these critters plotting to surprise.

So, in the shade of oaks so wide,
I'll laugh at my luck, with a bit of pride.
For even when trouble comes to play,
I'll choose to smile and sway away.

The Quiet Heart of the Pines

In the pines where the shadows creep,
There's a pinecone that dreams of deep sleep.
He rolls and he tumbles, quite the sight,
Saying, 'I'll nap till it's dark out tonight!'

The rabbits giggle, with noses a-twitch,
As they tease the cone, 'You're quite the rich!'
With dreams of grand feasts and nutty delight,
They hop on by, imagining the bite.

'A chipmunk's parade is coming, oh dear!'
Squeaked a twig, breaking silence so clear.
The cone shook with laughter; oh, what a thrill,
'What a show! I'll stick around, let's chill!'

So, ponder and chuckle in the soft shade,
Among dancing shadows, where joy is made.
With each little giggle, the forest has shown,
That rest is much sweeter when shared alone.

.

Serenade of the Bursting Seeds

The flowers are singing in colors bright,
While tulips giggle with sheer delight.
'Who will dance in the warm sunshine?'
The daisies squeal, 'Oh, it'll be divine!'

A dandelion sneezed, 'Oh, pardon me!'
And all the petals went flying free.
They twirled in the air, a whimsical race,
Laughing and spinning with flowery grace.

'Catch me if you can!' called a bold old stem,
As the bees buzzed close, joining the gem.
With pollen and laughter in all they spread,
The garden erupted, good vibes overhead.

And when the sky dimmed with shades of night,
The flowers nestled 'neath stars shining bright.
In slumber they whispered, 'What a sweet day!',
A serenade born from the joy of play.

Rhythms of the Woodland Path

On a path where the shadows sway and twist,
I stumbled on mushrooms that looked quite kissed.
'Who decorated you with dots so fine?'
Whispered a toad who just sipped on wine.

'Why are you here?' I curiously asked,
He chuckled, 'Enjoying? Why, that's my task!'
With each little hop, he sang a new tune,
Making even the flowers sway to the moon.

A parade of ants lined up in a row,
Marched past me, all ready for a show.
'We're off to the picnic, the sun's shining bright!'
I laughed at their hustle, such sweet little sights.

So I danced to the rhythm of rustling leaves,
Caught in the moment, the joy it weaves.
In the woodlands' embrace, I found my own laugh,
In the wild midst of nature, I trust the path.

In the Arms of the Arching Pines

In the shadow of tall trees, oh what a sight,
Squirrels host talent shows, they dance in delight.
A raccoon with a bowtie, plays lead in the band,
The audience of owls gives a round of hand.

Twisting trunked dancers sway with such grace,
Whispering secrets of their treetop place.
A gopher brings popcorn, he's quite the zest,
While a wandering bear steals the show—what a guest!

The pines stand tall, like grand halls of fame,
As critters conspire to create their own game.
Each branch tells a story, each leaf has a quip,
In this woodland circus, laughter won't skip.

So next time you're gazing up into the blue,
Remember the mayhem those critters pursue.
With each gust of wind, let your laughter cascade,
For life in the canopy's a jester's charade.

Inked Secrets of the Forest Floor

Beneath the tall trees where shadows blend,
Mushrooms hold meetings, there's laughter to send.
A beetle with glasses takes notes on the ground,
While ants form a chorus, their voices abound.

A fox tells tall tales of the critters he's seen,
His stories of rabbits, both clever and lean.
They giggle and chuckle, oh what a surprise,
A hedgehog in velvet, the sharpest of ties.

Twirling through grass, a dance of delight,
Grasshoppers join in, oh what a sight!
But wait, here comes a turtle, taking his time,
He stops for a snack, but it's all quite sublime.

So read the ground's parchment, let the secrets unfold,
In laughter and whimsy, nature's tales told.
With each pitter-patter and skittering sound,
A treasure of joy lies just under ground.

A Treetop's Tale Told in Verses

High above the bustle, where the air is sweet,
Parrots debate flavors of the fruit they eat.
A squirrel writes sonnets, and rabbits compose,
Their audience waiting in a bright, furry pose.

With acorns as props, the show takes a turn,
The beaver plays drums, watch the leaves start to churn!
Each branch turns a stage, each twig fits a rhyme,
In this wild musical, they've got the time.

A crow takes the lead, with a flair for the scene,
Dancing like a star, it's a sight so serene.
The fireflies wink, lighting the notes with their glow,
While the critters all chime in, putting on quite the show.

So if you're out wandering, beneath leafy gloves,
Listen for laughter, for the music it loves.
For up in the treetops, where the giggles reside,
A concert of nature is waiting inside.

Breaths of Sage and Shrubbery

In the breeze of the bushes, where the wild things dwell,
A coyote is singing, you can hear him quite well.
He howls to the moon, but with a twist of cheer,
A chorus of crickets join in for the smear.

The sagebrush rolls, like waves in the sea,
While a lizard in shades claims, "This throne belongs to me!"
Tumbleweeds tumble, like dancers they spin,
In a raucous assembly, let the fun times begin!

Rabbits in tuxedos hop 'round with pure glee,
Holding a tea party beneath the old tree.
A fox in a waistcoat brews coffee with flair,
While a butterfly wonders if she's landed on air.

So next in the shrubbery, don't pass by so quick,
Join the woodland party, it's quite the fun trick.
With breaths of fresh laughter, and whispers of cheer,
The sage and the shrub are all ready for sphere.

Ballads of the Whispering Woods

In the woods where squirrels play,
They dance and chatter all the day.
A raccoon sings with quite a flair,
While owls just hoot, as if they care.

The trees are tall; they laugh and sway,
As branches tickle, come what may.
The crows compose some silly tunes,
While frogs keep time with croaky croons.

A fox in boots struts down the lane,
He claims he's lost, but what's his gain?
With every leap, he trips and flips,
The rabbit giggles, while he slips.

So gather round, enjoy the show,
For mischief thrives where breezes blow.
The whispers here will make you grin,
In this wild world of giggles and spin.

Heartbeats Beneath the Canopy

In the shade where critters dwell,
A chipmunk's story, I must tell.
He hops around with acorns grand,
And juggles them with clumsy hands.

A quail in boots attempts to run,
But trips and falls—oh what fun!
The laughter echoes through the trees,
As squirrels snicker in the breeze.

With leaves that chuckle in the light,
The sun shines down, all warm and bright.
The shadows play like little sprites,
Tickling toes in woodland sights.

So listen close, you're in for a treat,
Under these branches, life's upbeat.
With every heartbeat, joy's reborn,
In nature's dance from night to morn.

Lament of the Lone Sequoia

Oh, mighty tree, you stand so tall,
But who's to hear your mighty call?
You sway in wind but often sigh,
Your friends are few, oh me, oh my!

A lizard sunbathes on your bark,
He claims that you're a famous park.
Yet here you stand, just all alone,
With whispers from the woods your scone.

You tell your tales to passing breeze,
Of ancient times and shifting leaves.
But every joke falls flat, it seems,
As critters giggle in their dreams.

So hold your head with noble grace,
In this kooky, leafy place.
Though laughter fades with setting sun,
You're still the tallest, oh so fun!

Wildflowers and Written Words

In a field of blooms where stories blend,
A dandelion declares, 'I'll mend!
I'll stitch together all I find,
With petals pure, and ties so kind.'

The bees compose a buzzing tune,
They write their notes by light of moon.
While butterflies laugh, in colors bright,
They flutter about with pure delight.

A snail recites his poem slow,
While daisies nod, 'Oh yes, we know!'
The whispers rustle in the breeze,
As laughter dances through the trees.

So gather flowers, write your rhyme,
In this meadow, joy's sublime.
With every word, a chuckle stirs,
In a world of tales, where fun occurs.

Dreamscapes of the Woodland Realm

In the forest, squirrels dance,
With acorns doing their prance.
Trees giggle, roots wiggle,
While critters in costumes jiggle.

Beneath the moon, the owls debate,
Who's the best at midnight skate?
With hats askew and feathers bright,
They take off on a laughter flight.

Foxes wear ties, lead a parade,
Barking tunes in the glade.
The pine trees sway to the sound,
Nature's joy simply unbound.

Oh, to join this silly spree,
Where every twig sings in glee!
With a wink and a nod, I'll say,
Let's dance 'til the light of day!

Fragments of a Forest Tale

Once a rabbit claimed a crown,
While the other critters frowned.
His carrot throne was quite a sight,
But he hopped left and lost his bite.

A bear barbecued in style,
Inviting raccoons, "Stay a while!"
The smoke rose high, the flames did twirl,
As the bees buzzed and did a whirl.

Chipmunks gathered for a feast,
With nuts and pies, they seemed the least.
But one slipped on a berry patch,
Flew into a laugh, what a match!

In this realm of woodland cheer,
Every critter gives a cheer.
With antics wild and hearts so free,
Nature's playground, where we agree!

Inked Between the Intertwined

Beneath the branches, shadows play,
As squirrels plot their thieving way.
With swipes so sly, and eyes so bright,
They steal the snacks of the owl's late night.

A tree stump whispered tales so tall,
Of mischief that befell them all.
The wise old owl just shook his head,
"Don't trust the forest's nightly bread!"

The flowers giggle, tulips sway,
Especially when bees go astray.
Buzzing loud but not quite right,
They land on friends in a fright.

Running and tumbling, hoot and holler,
The woodland's jokes ensure they'll wallow.
Laughter echoes through the glen,
In this realm where fun has no end!

The Cadence of Nature's Heartbeat

Crickets chirp their odd-ball tune,
While raccoons plot by the light of the moon.
A crow caws with an air so grand,
Demanding snacks from the nearby stand.

The brook babbles secrets, spills the beans,
As frogs croak out their marching scenes.
A turtle slow dances, sways his shell,
While the fireflies weave a glowing spell.

Oh, the antics of beasts at play,
From morning light to end of day.
In every leaf, there's laughter found,
In this woodland realm, joy does abound!

So let's raise a toast to nature's art,
With giggles and grins that warm the heart.
Together we'll laugh, sing, and roam,
In the woodland's embrace, we find our home!

Verses of the Old Forest

In the forest so ancient, a squirrel does glide,
With acorns in pockets, he tries to decide.
Should he hide them away, or just have a feast?
Every nut seems to giggle, oh what a beast!

A deer does ballet on the soft mossy ground,
While a bear takes a snooze, with snores that astound.
The trees are all chuckling, their branches a sway,
At the antics of critters who frolic and play.

The owl wears a monocle, sly and quite wise,
He hoots out some pointers, with twinkling eyes.
With branches all waving, the chorus takes flight,
In this funny old forest, the laughter feels right!

So wander through woods where the silliness flows,
You might catch a glimpse of a fox in fine clothes.
With tales of hilarity wrapped up in the trees,
Nature's own comic - it's sure to please!

Rhapsody of the Rustling Leaves

Leaves giggle and chatter, a musical crew,
They tickle the branches and laugh in the dew.
As the wind plays a tune, they twist and they twirl,
Inviting an acorn to join in the whirl.

A chipmunk in stripes does the cha-cha all day,
With a raccoon in sunglasses; now that's quite the play!
They host a grand dance on the forest floor,
Two-step with the shadows, who could ask for more?

Then a rabbit arrives, in a top hat so tall,
He trips and he tumbles, but still has a ball.
The trees rollick and rumble, their laughter so deep,
As beetles tap-dance, losing count as they leap.

In this rustling realm, where nature's a star,
Craziness reigns, and the shenanigans spar.
Join in if you dare, the fun never quits,
Where the leaves rustle sweetly, and humor befits!

Starlit Reflections on the Forest Floor

Under a blanket of stars, the critters convene,
An owl tells tall tales, no one knows what they mean.
The raccoons all giggle, with popcorn in hand,
As shadows bop along, making quite a stand.

Squirrels practice their dance in a flurry of glee,
While fireflies flash laughter, as bright as can be.
The night's full of mischief, and creatures galore,
Even the mushrooms seem ready for more!

With silver beams dancing on branches so high,
The critters make wishes as moments float by.
A deer's doing yoga, a bear sings a tune,
While frogs leap in rhythm beneath the full moon.

So venture, dear friend, to this starlit affair,
Where joy fills the shadows, and giggles fill air.
With every soft rustle, and gleam of the light,
The forest is buzzing with pure delight!

Haiku of the Mountain Breeze

Whispers through the pines,
A squirrel, dressed for a ball,
Chasing breezes, laughs.

Beetles tap their toes,
In rhythm with gusts that twirl,
Dance floor made of grass.

Clouds peek through the trees,
Mischief in their soft fluff,
Pinecones throw a bash.

Laughter fills the air,
Breezes join in the fun,
Nature's comedy!

Whispers of the Tall Pines

The pines gossip, oh what a sight,
They chuckle and wiggle, feeling light.
A squirrel in a suit shares a joke,
With a bear so fluffy, they both choke.

The owls wink, with wisdom in their eyes,
While chipmunks pretend to be sweet spies.
Each rustle of needles, a playful start,
Nature's own laugh, that tickles the heart.

Echoes Beneath the Canopy

Beneath the branches, a ruckus grows,
Can you hear the beat of nature's prose?
The shadowy limbs seem to dance and sway,
As if they're busting moves in a groovy way.

A rabbit moonwalks, quite out of tune,
While ants in a line form a conga swoon.
The echoes bounce, as laughter unfolds,
In this woodland stage where fun never molds.

Sonnet of the Swaying Needles

The needles sway like dancers in a trance,
Enjoying the rhythm of a rustling breeze,
They whisper secrets of mischief and chance,
While nearby a woodpecker eyeing the trees.

They gossip about critters and their stunts,
Squirrels in capes, leaping with flair,
A raccoon in shades planning late-night hunts,
In this silly glade, with laughter to spare.

The Silence of Sunlit Grove

In sunlit groves, the shadows are sly,
Where laughter festers and giggles lie.
A deer does ballet on mossy soft ground,
While frogs croak a tune, making fun all around.

The sunbeams tickle the bark of the trees,
As they share tales of their age-old decrees.
With every rustle, a chuckle erupts,
At the antics of nature, everyone erupts.

Sonnet Under the Starry Boughs

Beneath the branches, squirrels play,
They plot, they scheme, in their nutty way.
With acorns stashed, they dance around,
While moonlit laughter fills the ground.

A wise old owl on a branch so high,
Tilts his head to watch them fly.
"Do they know," he hoots with glee,
"Tomorrow's storm will set them free?"

The stars above twinkle in time,
As critters dream of their next big climb.
"Who needs a plan?" the badger grins,
"I'll just dig deep for winter wins!"

So under the sky and leafy sheets,
Life bustles on with hearty feats.
The forest hums a quirky tune,
As mischief reigns beneath the moon.

The Council of Quiet Pines

In a clearing wide, the pines convene,
Discussing whispers and what they mean.
"Who took my shade?" a young sapling cries,
"I swear it was right, under bright skies!"

The oldest pine clears his throat with care,
"It's just the wind, you can't stay bare.
We've all lost needled bits, my friend,
But don't fret, this is just the trend."

A chipmunk jokes, "Pineapples wouldn't grow,
In this setting, it's just too slow!"
The crowd erupts with rustling laughter,
And peace returns soon after the banter.

So they laugh and sway in the gentle breeze,
While making sure none of them freeze.
Together they stand, strong and bright,
In their green council, everything's just right.

Chronicles of the Green Haven

In the kingdom of bark, where shadows play,
A tale unfolds in a funny way.
The fox went to court for his missing tail,
"Who took it?" he asked with a furious wail.

The rabbits giggled, "Just borrow some glue,
We'll stick it right back, it'll look good as new!"
But the judge, a sly tortoise, just shook his head,
"Let's have a dance-off, or you'd best be dead!"

The dancing commenced, it was quite a sight,
With twirls and hops under the moonlight.
"A tail's just a tail, let it freely sway,
Or find a new one in some other way!"

Finally, the fox, in joyful cheer,
Found a new tail, right near his ear.
In the haven of green, they learned that day,
Laughter and friendship are the best way to play.

Inked Leaves and Twilight Dreams

With inked leaves fluttering, secrets unfold,
Scribbled tales of the brave and bold.
A beetle wrote poems, so tattered and torn,
About his adventures from dusk until morn.

"Your rhymes are a mess!" said the wise firefly,
"Stick to the light, don't let your dreams die!"
But the beetle just shrugged, "At least I have flair,
One day, I'll dazzle, I promise, I swear!"

As twilight painted the sky in hues,
The critters gathered, sharing their views.
"Let's write our stories, don't leave them alone,
Every leaf has wisdom, each poem a tone!"

So they scribbled and giggled, beneath twilight's glow,
In a world of ink, where imagination flows.
With laughter spreading like wildfire's gleam,
Inked leaves reveled in their wildest dreams.

Lyrical Lullabies Among the Pines

Beneath the trees, the squirrels prance,
A dance of nuts, a furry dance.
The birds all laugh, they chirp and sing,
As frogs in hats debate the spring.

The owls wear glasses, wise and round,
While raccoons dig in mounds of sound.
A deer in boots hops with delight,
As fireflies sparkle through the night.

The pines sway gently in the breeze,
Their needles whisper riddles, tease.
A bear just yawns, a sleepy grin,
In dreams of honey, he dives right in.

So gather close, and hear the cheer,
Of nature's jesters gathered near.
In every rustle, laugh, and quirk,
The woods invite us all to work.

Elderwood's Enchanted Verses

The gnomes wear shoes with floppy toes,
While mockingbirds steal half their clothes.
A breeze that tickles leaves so bright,
Starts a duel with a blushing light.

In hidden nooks, the critters meet,
To share their snacks and swap their feet.
A squirrel recites a rodent rhyme,
As badgers dance in perfect time.

The maples giggle with their leaves,
As beetles boast of their grand heaves.
A mystic tree with wisdom so wide,
Advises all with gleeful pride.

And while the shadows start to creep,
The whispers in the woods do leap.
In elderwood, where laughter reigns,
The joyous heart forever gains.

Nature's Anthems in Amber Glow

The sun dips low, a golden show,
As crickets chirp in concert glow.
A raccoon juggles acorns high,
While fireflies flicker in the sky.

The evening breeze—oh what a tease!
It lifts the hats of bumblebees.
The owls hoot tune from trees up tall,
While hedgehogs don their spiky pall.

A river sings a river's tune,
While turtles dance beneath the moon.
The shadows play their game of chase,
As laughter fills the quiet space.

In amber glow, nature's delight,
Unfolds its stories, pure and bright.
Where every creature finds its place,
And chuckles echo, filling space.

Pondering Places of Profound Reflection

On mossy stones, I sit and muse,
As otters roam, they'll never lose.
A stoic turtle gives advice,
"Slow and steady, that's quite nice."

The frogs debate their raucous song,
While crickets trill along so strong.
A wise old owl, with knowing eyes,
Predicts tomorrow's weather skies.

Through rustling leaves, bright colors gleam,
As nature fills the mind with dream.
A subtle giggle stirs the air,
With every critter's playful flair.

So with a chuckle, share this spot,
For pondering joy is what you ought.
In vibrant woods, both wild and free,
The heart finds laughter, wild with glee.

Musings Among the Moss

In the forest a squirrel took flight,
Chasing a leaf in a whimsical plight.
It leaped with a flare, did a twirl in the air,
Landed in moss with a thump, what a sight!

A wise old owl hooted with glee,
Watching the squirrel, such a sight to see.
"You think you're so grand,
But you're not in command,
Nature's the maestro, let it be!"

Frogs croaked along, adding their song,
While ants marched in line, they couldn't go wrong.
With a comical croon,
Beneath the bright moon,
The critters rejoiced, just singing along!

So next time you wander, take heed of the play,
Nature's a stage for the silly display.
With a giggle and cheer,
Invite you to steer,
Dance with the critters, let merriment stay!

Rhymes of Resin and Rest

Beneath the tall trees, a pinecone sat tight,
Wishing to roll, but it just wasn't right.
"Oh, how I'd roll,
If I had some whole
Momentum, like leaves when they take flight!"

A beetle nearby joined the chatter so bold,
"You pinecone, my friend, you're so stubborn, behold!
Just give it a shove,
Feel the pure love,
Life's fun when you're not just feeling old!"

The sun laughed along, casting shadows so rare,
While mushrooms below wiggled, tossing their hair.
"Let's lunch on some dew,
While we're feeling new,
And dance like nobody loves a good scare!"

So gather your friends in the forest so sweet,
Where laughter can echo with every heartbeat.
In the sun or the rain,
There's joy to gain,
Just let the fun flow, and life's a treat!

Nature's Lyrical Embrace

A rabbit with dreams of becoming a star,
Told tales to the trees about traveling far.
"I'll hop and I'll dance,
With a cool up-and-down prance,
Join me, dear friends! You don't need a guitar!"

The leaves all chuckled, swaying with glee,
"You silly old rabbit, a star you could be!
But stay in your lane,
Or it might be a pain,
To chase fame while munching on clover, tee-hee!"

A raccoon chimed in with a bright shiny wink,
"You think you're the best? Well, come on, let's think!
Let's host a grand show,
With a nose to the toe,
We'll see who can sing and who can just stink!"

With laughter and song, the forest did glow,
Critters gathered 'round, putting on quite the show.
So if you feel low,
Just let it all flow,
Join the woodland dance and watch your heart grow!

Shadows Danced in Dappled Light

In the dappled glow, shadows start to twirl,
A clumsy old frog in a fashionable whirl.
"Watch me, I'm fab,
Though a bit of a drab,
I'm ribbiting rumors, give them a whirl!"

The butterflies giggled, flapping their wings,
"Oh dear little friend, how you do pull the strings!
But don't go too far,
You're not a rock star,
Just a jester in nature, with all of your flings!"

A hedgehog nearby rolled right into play,
"Let's start a parade, come what may!"
With a hop and a skip,
They began to equip,
The forest with joy and a silly ballet!

So if you're feeling low in the wild,
Remember the laughter, the fun of the child.
Join in with delight,
Dancing shadows at night,
Together in nature, forever beguiled!

Reveries of Roots and Rain

In the forest there's a tree,
Its roots dance like a bumblebee.
They trip and tumble in soft brown earth,
Claiming the land, declaring their worth.

The raindrops giggle from the sky,
Splashing leaves where squirrels fly.
A puddle forms with a fleeting jig,
The frogs leap in, doing a little wig.

Mushrooms sprout like unexpected hats,
While the snails engage in casual chats.
The wind tickles branches, makes them sway,
As if the trees just heard a joke today.

Nature's antics never cease,
Every rustle hints at some comedic piece.
With laughter ringing 'neath the leafy reign,
The forest thrives on its roots and rain.

Ephemeral Elegies in the Underbrush

In thickets small, a critter prances,
Hopping 'round like it's taken chances.
A lizard slips, a shadowed brief,
Its antics leave the bugs in disbelief.

Amongst the leaves, a joke was spun,
A caterpillar running just for fun.
But then it paused, said, "I must go,
I'm late for lunch—there's fungus in tow!"

The beetles gather for a grand soirée,
While ants bring snacks to the buffet.
With tiny forks, they toast the day,
To fleeting moments in a silly play.

In this underbrush, life knows no bounds,
Every rustle offers whimsical sounds.
Though time can tease, each laugh won't linger,
They wave goodbye with a giggling finger.

Wanderlust Within the Wilderness

Amidst the trees, a squirrel's quest,
To find the nut that's simply the best.
With acorn maps and a tiny hat,
He struts along, fancy like a aristocrat.

The brook babbles, with tales to share,
Of frogs in tuxedos and fish with flair.
"Why swim upstream?" asked one such trout,
"Let's kick back here, let the world figure out!"

The breeze whispers secrets, oh so light,
"Ever seen a raccoon that can dance just right?"
Under the stars, where the wild ones play,
Wanderlust lives in a comical way.

As creatures lounge, they dream and scheme,
Planning adventures in nature's dream.
Those wild antics, through shade and sun,
Make every day an outrageous run.

Whispers in the Wildflower Meadow

Wildflowers bloom with a giggly glare,
Each petal whispers, "You can't compare!"
Bees buzz around with their busy talk,
"Did you smell that? It's great as a walk!"

Butterflies flutter in costume so bright,
Debating which flower looks just right.
"Let's have a ball!" one says with glee,
As they twirl in the air, wild and free.

The breeze plays tricks, tugging their dress,
As they stumble in a flurry of nonsense.
"Caught in a gust!" they scream and they dart,
Falling in laughter, that's the true art.

In the meadow's embrace, fun never ends,
Nature's jesters are truly great friends.
With every chuckle and playful sway,
Life's wildflower party is here to stay!

www.ingramcontent.com/pod-product-compliance
Lightning Source LLC
Chambersburg PA
CBHW071850160426
43209CB00003B/492